OH MY GOD, I'M 40!

THE 40-SOMETHING WOMAN'S SURVIVAL GUIDE

Crombie Jardine
PUBLISHING LIMITED
Office 2, 3 Edgar Buildings
George Street, Bath, BA1 2FJ
www.crombiejardine.com
www.twitter.com/crombiejardine

First published in 2010
by Crombie Jardine Publishing Limited
Copyright © Deborah Durbin, 2010

ISBN 978-1-906051-46-4

Written by Deborah Durbin

Printed and bound in China

CONTENTS

You know you're 40 when...
your idea of a good time is sitting in
the garden, drinking a nice Sauvignon
blanc and reading the papers.

INTRODUCTION

*The first sign of maturity is the discovery
that the volume knob also turns to the left*

Jerry M. Wright

You know it's coming. You've been putting it off for as long as you can. Despite telling yourself that you're no different and that it's only another year, that little voice inside your head is telling you otherwise; saying things like, 'Oh, My God, I'm getting OLD!'

There's no denying it, it's a bitter pill to swallow. To suddenly go from a young-and-funky-30-something that frequented Glastonbury every year to someone who now collects Sainsbury's Active Kids vouchers in such an enthusiastic manner is positively scary.

The realization that you have reached the stage in your life where it is considered unacceptable to have anything other than your ears pierced, get offensively drunk or wear combat trousers à la All Saints, is one of shock and disbelief.

You suddenly realize that you will no longer be able to identify with the cast from *Friends*, people will expect you to not only have a mortgage but also a pension plan and several ISAs tucked up your sleeve and you will start thinking about what tracks you want played at your funeral. Is it any wonder if you're feeling depressed?

There was a time when 40 seemed like a million miles away and then suddenly the countdown is on and before you know it, it's upon you in all its taupe glory.

Unfortunately, no amount of pretending it's not happening to you and that you are forever 39 is going to make things better. It's all very well if you're blessed with good genes and are lucky enough to look ten years younger than you actually are, but even this has its down side: you will never escape that mocking voice inside your head that screams in the dead of night, "Sensible shoes and bingo wings!"

In a bid to cling to the last vestige of a young 30-something, many women will lie about their age. This is not advisable. It is one thing to try and convince yourself but quite another to insist to others that you are still eligible to tick the 29-35 box on the National Census. And this will only result in having to lie about everything that has ever happened in your life up until now. For instance: you will no longer be able to sing along to *Too Shy* by Kajagoogoo for fear of someone asking how you happen to know not only all the words but all the dance moves too; you will also have to amend the kids' birth certificates, which apparently is illegal, and you will have to refrain from being quite so enthusiastic about watching *Coronation Street* and even give this up in favour of *Hollyoaks* if you are going to convince anyone that you are younger than your years.

It's all very well for Madonna to don thigh-length leather boots and a black basque. She's a multi-millionaire and multi-millionaires can wear whatever they like, whatever their age... However, the average 40-year-old woman, on the other hand, will have to think very carefully about how she dresses to avoid being poked and pointed at by kids (not to mention parents) in the playground.

Unfortunately, nothing other than denial can prevent you from turning 40, but with the help of *Oh My God, I'm 40! The 40-Something Woman's Survival Guide* you will be adequately prepared to face the big Four-O head on and revel in the simple things in the 40-something woman's life, such as being able to look smug when you hand over a ten pound note and the odd change to an obnoxious

16-year-old shop assistant and watch with relish as she tries to work out how much to give you back, and officially write letters of complaint to everyone who has ever crossed your path...

Age is an issue of mind over matter.
If you don't mind, it doesn't matter

Mark Twain

CHAPTER 1

THE OH CRIKEY! COUNTDOWN

You know you're 40 when...
you start getting on very well with
your doctor.

The Oh Crikey! Countdown is the feeling that every 39-year-old woman will get. Yes, you know the one: that sudden realization that not only do you not get the latest music but that you find yourself re-tuning the car radio from Radio One to Radio Two due to the fact that the 'Chart' music sounds much like a cat trapped in a washing machine.

The Oh Crikey! Countdown includes common feelings and inexplicable urges that every 39-year-old will feel as she approaches the big Four-O and these are dealt with here...

The inexplicable urge to write your funeral wishes

Whilst it's best probably not to make a big deal of this, it needs to be mentioned... One of the most common feelings as you approach your 40th birthday is the subject of your own mortality and working out how many years you have left and, more importantly, who you want to read your eulogy at your funeral. Yes, this is quite common as you approach the milestone that no woman wants to approach. You will find that you go from being a woman who took chances, drank too much, accepted lifts from virtual strangers (not to mention often sleeping with them), ate what she wanted and basically challenged death on a daily basis to someone who refuses to go out after dark for fear of being mugged by a hoodie, falls over after two shandies, gets fat just by looking at a Flake and when sleeping with someone actually goes to sleep. You will also spend a lot of time sitting up in bed contemplating health issues, the force of gravity, death and, more importantly, your own demise.

Yes, if you are approaching 40 you can expect to spend many days collecting the Axa Sun Life Funeral Plan flyers that frequently fall out of the Sunday supplements and writing down specific instructions as to what type of coffin you wish to be buried in, who you do and definitely don't want to come to your funeral, what colours the bereaved should be dressed in and what type of flowers you would prefer.

Having spent too many hours watching *Casualty* you will spend many more hours contemplating your demise from this world. A road traffic accident on the way home from a trip to Marks & Spencer?

A fall down the stairs as you trip over your bingo-wings? Or maybe you will dare to venture out in the evening and foolishly tackle the hoodie who is vandalizing your car and fall over, bang your head and never come out of your coma?

Having contemplated your funeral you will then leave a copy of your 'should-anything-happen-to-me' funeral requests (including heart-wrenching letters to your loved-ones) everywhere just in case you suddenly pop your clogs in the middle of the night.

The inexplicable urge to watch furniture adverts

Or any advert that displays a combination of a sofa
and an ex-member of *EastEnders* for that matter...

This urge is a strange one, but one that is very
common in women who are about to turn, or have
just turned, 40. It's a bit like trying to understand the
laws of gravity or the laws of Sod; you know they are
there, you just don't know why. There you are one
minute with not a care in the world – and quite
frankly couldn't give a monkey's what furniture you
sat on – and the next minute you're glued to the TV,
nodding in agreement as Martin Kemp tells you how
you can save on sofa beds and also get four years'
interest free credit to boot – result!

The inexplicable urge to wear taupe

Another of life's weird and wonderful mysteries of the 40-something is the urge to suddenly start wearing taupe, or any colour that is a member of the swamp-brown family: mushroom, coffee, fawn, camel, beige, buff, it's all the same to me. As you approach your forties the desire to visit the 'Classics' section in Marks & Spencer is somewhat overwhelming and try as you might to avoid the store by wearing a bag over your head and running past the shop as quickly as your sensible shoes will take you, it's no good, you will be drawn in through the automatic doors by the magnetism that is Twiggy in all her taupe glory.

The inexplicable urge to write endless letters of complaint

As you approach 40 you will discover the overwhelming and inexplicable urge for justice in the world and this will involve many hours of dedicating your time to writing letters of complaint to anyone and everyone – regardless of whether or not they deserve it. The snotty cashier at the supermarket will be victimized for trying to keep the free carrier bags hidden under her desk, continually snarling at you and hinting that you should buy another 'Bag for Life' as she scans your groceries. The postman will be reprimanded for failing to push the post right through the letter box and you'll report your GP to the General Medical Council for giving the elderly patient in front of you more than ten minutes of his time, despite the fact that he had just suffered a heart attack in the surgery waiting room. Oh yes, whereas before you would just shrug and maybe stick two fingers up to these minor annoyances, now anyone and everyone who crosses you will soon know about it in the form of a letter of complaint.

There are numerous other symptoms of the soon-to-be-40-woman, many of which you will only have to look at your mother to see. The only advice I can offer is to just ride with it. Plan your funeral, watch as many furniture adverts as you wish, give in to Twiggy and get the Basildon Bond out. I assure you this phase will pass.

The Manager
Marks & Spencer
Taupe Road
Somewhere in the UK

Dear Sir,

I am writing to complain about the lack of beige in your Autumn collection this year. As a woman who has recently developed an inexplicable passion for taupe, I was saddened to discover that your entire poncho range extended to only two shades: Moroccan Camel and Chocolate Heaven.

Whilst I am a big fan of both hues, I do feel that the presence of additional shades would benefit customers who would like more variety to what is essentially an item of clothing that every woman should have in their wardrobe.

I trust that you will take my comments on board and introduce more variety into your next collection.

Yours faithfully,
A 40-something Woman

The aging process has you firmly in its grasp if you never get the urge to throw a snowball

Doug Larson

CHAPTER 2

THE BIG DAY

You know you're 40 when...
it takes twice as long to look half
as good.

Yes, no matter how long you put it off, that day is going to arrive, whether you like it or not. There's no escaping it. You can't hide it down the side of the sofa like that empty multipack of Aeros, you know. The 40th birthday is as guaranteed as day follows night, so you might just as well take advantage of it. There are two ways of successfully doing this:

The tell-the-world technique

This involves announcing to the world (or just your family and friends if you don't want to look like the mad cat woman from *The Simpsons*) that you are approaching your 40th birthday. If you play your cards right, you might even be up for the Oscar nominations – see, I told you it wasn't that bad.

Now, the advantage of the tell-the-world-technique is that as women are known for being somewhat unpredictable, and as everyone knows how touchy we are about our age, no one will take the chance of upsetting you for fear of finding you rocking back and forth, crying hysterically in the bathroom. Any man faced with the prospect of a hysterically hormonal woman will recoil at this thought and do everything he can to ensure that your milestone birthday will be one to remember for all the right reasons.

Guaranteed, at the mere mention of your 40th birthday there will be chocolate a-plenty, flowers, candles, baths with scented oils prepared and you won't have to do a stitch of housework for weeks, maybe even months if you can put in an award winning performance.

The tell-the-world technique – Part Two: Announcement-through-a-megaphone

Whilst the tell-the-world technique does the job of ensuring that your day will be one of wonderment and joy, the announcement-through-a-megaphone technique is equally effective and doesn't include having to attend a single acting class.

This technique requires a bit of planning: First of all you will need the appropriate equipment – one megaphone. Secondly, you will need to find a venue where a lot of people gather, for example a shopping centre. Failing that, a football ground on a Saturday afternoon will suffice.

Armed with your megaphone, you announce loudly to all and sundry that it is your 40th birthday. By doing this you will a) gain sympathy from every woman on the planet that has heard you and b)

get the required attention from your
husband/boyfriend/significant other who will
think, "Oh, Christ, I'd better be really, extra-specially
nice to her and get her something she really wants
this time for her birthday."

Even strangers will congratulate/empathize with
you and will often give you free stuff. For example,
for weeks coming up to my 40th I casually dropped
into every conversation that my milestone birthday
was looming, resulting in several free bottles of
wine from the local curry house, a box of Milk Tray
from the newsagents, flowers from the florist,
three free tins of Whiskers from the local grocer
(the fact that I don't own a cat didn't really matter;
it was the thought that counted) and a whole
sheep from the local farmer. I still haven't figured
out quite what to do with the sheep, but like I say,
it's the thought that counts.

With a bit of planning you can dedicate entire weeks to dropping hints about your 40th birthday and with a bit of luck you will be knee deep in gifts by the time the event actually takes place. It's probably best not to mention it to the local farmer, though, unless you want to be knee deep in sheep casserole for the rest of your life.

Youth is a wonderful thing.
What a crime to waste it on children

George Bernard Shaw

CHAPTER 3

NOW YOU ARE 40, WHAT YOU CAN EXPECT

You know you're 40 when...

6:00 a.m. is when you get up, not
when you go to sleep.

The best way to get through the milestone birthday that is your 40th is, in my opinion, to drink yourself into a stupor and when you eventually wake up (probably several weeks later), all being well, your mind and body will have (hopefully) adjusted from being a young-and-happening-30-something to a Jesus-I-feel-old-40-something. So what can you expect now? And what will other people expect from you?

You will be expected to have a mortgage

It was quite acceptable, even somewhat cool in fact, to not have any ties when you were in your thirties. You were considered to be a free-spirit, an urban warrior, a freethinker, refusing to conform and contribute to the capitalism of the world. You were a maverick and slightly rebellious for refusing to give in to the demands of society. Damn it, you were cool! And then what happens? No sooner have you blown out your 40 candles than you are expected to not only have a mortgage, a pension and several ISAs up your sleeve, but you are also expected to be well versed in the difference between a flat rate mortgage and an endowment mortgage and whether you should have a stakeholder pension or go for the occupational defined contribution scheme. Que?

I mean, Jesus, how are you meant to know these things? And what happened to the I'm-never-going-to-fall-into-that-economic-capitalist-ideology anarchistic view that we had in our twenties and thirties?

Now that you're a 40-something, it is assumed that you will have abandoned your dreams of being a free-spirit, travelling around the world armed with little more than a rucksack, a pair of flip-flops and a handful of Euros. You are expected to discard any dreams you once had of sharing a house with the other *X Factor* contestants or auditioning to go on next year's *Big Brother*. Oh, no, the moment you jump from being a 30-something to a 40-something, you are expected to... well, act and behave like a grown-up.

Not only must you now have a mortgage, a pension plan and several ISAs, you must have a 'proper' job, take only one holiday per year, and watch 'grown-up' programmes such as *Working Lunch* and *Newsnight* rather than *Loose Women* and repeats of *Desperate Housewives*. By now you should be able to bake a cake à la Nigella Lawson, know how to darn a sock, competently carry out a funeral fitting for a pet rabbit, understand what a stopcock is and, more importantly, know where to find it and how to turn it off without phoning a friend or going 50/50, know the shrinkage difference between washing a woollen jumper at 30 degrees and 50 degrees, know how much Calpol is too much Calpol and be acquainted with nit-removal techniques.

Yes, as soon as you hit 40, you are expected to act and behave like a grown-up. The solution to this? Well, you can either accept it gracefully and buy a copy of *Mortgages for Dummies*, and Nigella's latest bestseller, or you can stick two fingers up to society and let someone else, like your mother, continue to advise you on the appropriate way to wash a woolly jumper and be a domestic goddess. I, personally, favour the latter.

Your body will change drastically

And if that's not bad enough, you can also expect
your once toned and nymph-like body to change to
a very alarming degree. Like a moth to a flame, you
will be drawn to the hair and beauty aisle in the
supermarket in a bid to exterminate the prominent
wiry grey hairs that seems to have sprouted
overnight. Be thankful they are just on your head
for now.

However, having never had the need to buy
anything with the sentence '100% grey coverage'
written on it before, you will be faced with the
challenge of applying hair colourant successfully so
that you still have that natural look and don't end
up looking like a reject from a Toyah Wilcox tour.

Another section of the hair and beauty aisle that
you will frequent on a regular basis will be the one

where they stock hugely expensive anti-wrinkle creams due to the fact that those laughter lines under your eyes no longer disappear when you stop laughing and your face now looks as though a crow has come up in the night and stamped all over it. The words of your mother will come back to haunt you... "Moisturise, moisturise, moisturise!"

You will have to try harder

If you're already married with kids, you will discover a strange phenomenon occurring in the school playground as other 40-something women try to outdo you in the look-at-me-I'm-40-and-still-gorgeous stakes. Just because you're paranoid doesn't mean they aren't out to get you.

You can no longer fall out of the house with that I-just-tumbled-out-of-bed-look of sweat-pants and t-shirt. It looked kind of cute when you were in your thirties. Those sweat pants are now leisure pants and there is a subtle difference. Now it will look as though you've given up on your looks and your life and let it run riot. And with so many yummy-mummies to compete with, you are going to have to get up much much earlier just to pluck, push and pummel everything back into place in order to look half decent when you drop off your kids at school.

You will also realize that if you had to take your driving test again you would fail because you can't see two foot in front of you, let alone the 20.5 metres in good daylight requirement for a driving test. Thankfully, it is still considered trendy to wear glasses without looking like a total loser, but do remember that your prescription glasses are no longer a fashion statement, but a necessity if you are to pick up the right child from school. It can be rather embarrassing, not to mention disconcerting, to get home and suddenly realize that your child must still be standing in the playground because, having found your specs, you seem to have adopted a small person who looks nothing like you or your husband.

Still single?

And what, Heaven forbid, if you're not married and settled down with children by the time you're 40? Well, you might just as well give up now!

If you're not settled down in cosy coupledom by the time you hit 40, then instead of thinking how cool you are to be able to travel anywhere in the world with just a rucksack, as was the case when you were in your thirties, people will just think you're now a sad old spinster and may suggest you adopt a cat for companionship, seeing as you can't find a man to settle down with.

And what if you do want to find a man when you're 40? Where on Earth do you find one that doesn't come with baggage? The clubs you frequented when you were in your twenties are full of, well, 20-somethings and the only people in your age-range that go there are mad women who own lots of cats.

'They' say that the best way for a 40-something woman to find an available man is either to go to a speed-dating event or have a bash at internet dating. I'm not so sure.

Speed dating

These events are usually found in country pubs in the middle of nowhere and as a rule have been dreamt up by some well meaning landlady who thinks she's a cross between Cilla Black and Cupid and is doing her bit for the world by bringing together lonely souls. In reality it's the chance for one-eyed farmers, far and wide, to have the remotest chance of pulling someone that doesn't look like the back end of a sheep. I wouldn't bother if I were you. You will just spend the night thinking up excuses to leave and trying not to look aghast when for the third time that evening his glass eye drops out into his pint.

Internet dating

You've heard the story; lonely 40-something woman, looking for love, meets handsome, charming, single man on the internet. They fall in love, get married and sell their story to *Take-a-Break!*

In reality the handsome Prince Charming is a 56-year-old, balding social misfit with a penchant for dodgy internet forums and you have discovered that he has pitched his tent outside your house because, despite all the warnings and normally being of sound mind, you inadvertently believed him when he asked for your address so that he could send you the red rose he had grown especially for you.

You will also discover that rather than looking very much like Sawyer from *Lost* and living in a spacious loft apartment, actually he looks more like Hurley and lives in Dudley with his mother and many cats.

The problem is that if you have given out your home address and/or telephone number, and the farmer is persistent, you will need some excuses ready to avoid going out on date number two. These excuses need to be pretty lame – the aim is to get the point across – but effective – in a not-too-antagonistic way. The good thing is that now you've hit 40 you can say things you wouldn't have dreamt of when you were in your twenties and thirties. Here are some rubbish excuses to chose from:

- *I have to wash my dog*

- *I have to floss my cat*

- *The man on television told me to say tuned*

- *I'm teaching my ferret to yodel*

- *I have to check the sell-by dates on my tins*

- *I'm converting my calendar from Julian to Gregorian*

- *My plot to take over the world is thickening*

- *I have to fulfil my potential*

- *My subconscious says no*

- *Mother would never let me hear the end of it*

- *It wouldn't be fair to the other Beautiful People if I went out with you*

- *The voices in my head are telling me to stay away from you*

- *I think I'm a closet gay*

What's wrong with being 40 and single, anyway?

If you happen to have made it this far and have yet to find Mr Right, celebrate! For starters, you get to have a huge grown-up bed all to yourself. Being married is like going back to your childhood and having to share a room with your annoying little sister. Much like siblings, married people have to share a room and a bed, whether they like it or not. Wouldn't it be great to have your own room again where the only pants you had to pick up were your own and if you wanted to cover the ceiling in fairy-lights, you damn well could?

Another bonus of being 40 and single is that you are able to go into a supermarket and come out with only the things you want – mainly chocolate and wine – and not a bumper bag of Haribos, and several Kinder Eggs.

You will hear tick-tock all the time

Men. They may think they rule the world, but they don't and unfortunately for us it is women that have been designed to reproduce and have babies. If you are a 40-something woman and you don't already have kids, then you can be sure that the noise you keep hearing is not two Chinese men playing ping-pong; it is your biological clock ticking like a time-bomb. Ignore it if you must but by the time you enter your forties, your biological clock alters in sound from a background ticking to an orchestrally-challenged version of the River Dance.

As much as you would like to continue in your fabulous career, because men can't (and wouldn't even if they could) produce their own offspring, Mother Nature has a habit of turning us into baby-obsessed drivelling maniacs if we haven't yet produced a mini-me as soon as we hit 40 and a good job too, really, because if she didn't the world would come to a resounding halt.

If you are faced with the feeling that Michael Flatley is doing an Irish jig in your head on a daily basis, do yourself a favour and agree to procreate with that one-eyed farmer. It will shut up Mother Nature for five minutes. Just don't give out your address...

CHAPTER 4

WHAT NOT TO WEAR WHEN YOU ARE 40

You know you're 40 when...

you don't try and hold your stomach in, no matter who walks by.

A year ago you could still get away with wearing a pair of combat trousers and a t-shirt with a humorous slogan across your chest. Now that you are no longer a 30-something, but a 40-something, you will look like an All Saints reject just trying to recapture her youth. Unfair I know, but hey, that's life.

So, in light of the transition, and feeling a Trinny and Susannah moment coming on, I feel it is only fair to point out what you can and cannot get away with wearing when you are a 40-something...

What not to wear

Anything with gold on it
Victoria Beckham can get away with it because
she's Victoria Beckham and she has her own brand
of perfume – oh, and she isn't 40 yet. You, on the
other hand, will end up looking like a cross
between Dame Shirley Bassey and Lilly Savage.

Any t-shirt with a humorous slogan on it
This will only encourage people to look at your
breasts and notice how far south they've gone.

Anything with an animal print on it
Kate Moss can get away with it because she's still
young and beautiful. You can't because you will
look as brassy as a middle-aged barmaid – think a
cross between Peggy Mitchell and Bet Lynch.

Thongs
If, like me, you have a bum the size of Wales, a
thong just does not look good. In fact it is quite
positively scary to catch a glimpse of a 40-
something's bum in a thong. Don't do it, you'll only
embarrass yourself and those around you.

A bikini
And in particular, a thong bikini. Not only will your
bum look like a lump of cheese on a cheeseboard,
that jelly-belly you got as a result of having the
ungrateful kids will make you look like you already
have a rubber ring around your waist. No, ladies,
leave the bikini at home. You owe it to yourself and
to your dignity.

Shorts skirts and low tops
No-one wants to see your varicose veins or the
stretch marks on your boobs from the hours of
breastfeeding the unappreciative kids. Madonna

and Cher might be able to pull it off, just, but you are neither Madonna nor Cher, so please stop pretending that you are.

What to wear

Given that we now look ridiculous in anything that is short, trendy, sparkly or thong-like, it's little wonder that we 40-somethings are drawn to the doors of Marks & Spencer in a bid to clothe ourselves and protect what little dignity we have left. Here follows a list of what is considered suitable attire for the 40-something woman:

Anything in that bland taupey, camelly, runny poo colour is a good place to start
Yes, I know it looks like you couldn't be bothered when you got out of bed this morning and you will resemble Pauline Fowler from *EastEnders*, but at least you will complement the living room walls –

after all, the 40-something's house is expected to be painted from top to bottom in magnolia, not the fuchsia pink you would love it to be.

Anything with a polo-neck
This will hide those giveaway, scraggy chicken neck signs that every 40-something woman will succumb to overnight.

A poncho
The ultimate investment every 40-something woman should have in her wardrobe. The poncho will be your friend. It will hide a multitude of sins: jelly-belly, sagging boobs, not to mention the bingo wings that will develop during the night. You can also have hours of fun saying things like, "Make my day, punk."

Magic pants
A pair of these will instantly shrink your stomach, making you look as though you really do get your money's worth with that gym membership that you took out in January. The only downfall is that the fat has to go somewhere, so you will either develop an extra set of thighs or boobs. Either way this is easily combated by wearing a taupe poncho over the top.

CHAPTER 5

THE DISADVANTAGES OF BEING 40

You know you're 40 when...
a £3.50 bottle of wine is no longer
'pretty good stuff'.

Aside from the fact that you will have to change your entire wardrobe, your kids will hate you and you will be expected to behave like a responsible grown-up, there are a number of other changes I feel it only fair to warn you about:

Loss of respect

You will also have to contend with the loss of respect at home, and, well, everywhere really, when you become a 40-something. Anyone that once had an ounce of respect for you when you were 39 will about turn and treat you with utter contempt as soon as you hit your milestone birthday.

Your junk mail will no longer be open invites to raves or wild 18-30s holidays. No. Rather, you will start to receive brochures for Haven family holidays and information leaflets explaining step by step how to bleed your radiators, all of which you will find interesting. You will also find that cashiers will refer to you as "madam" and not "miss" – don't be fooled, this is not a mark of respect, rather the opposite – they know you're past it.

Saggy bottom and baggy bingo wings

Another disadvantage that the 40-something will have to contend with is the 40-something derrière. That once pert and peachy bum you had in your thirties will, without warning, quickly upon turning 40 turn into an arse the size of a small town house. There is nothing you can do about this and no amount of discreet squeezing your buttocks in the queue in Sainsbury's will bring back the pert peachiness you were once proud to put on display in a thong. Discreet buttock squeezing exercises will only serve to make you look as though you are practising for a gurning contest. Added to this, your once Madonnaesque muscle-toned arms will grow small, flabby wings, otherwise known as bingo-wings, dinner-lady arms, or (rather cruelly, I think) nanna-wobbles. Unfortunately, this is another one of those unexplained mysteries sent to try us and no amount of push-ups will give you back the biceps of your youth.

You could try joining a gym class to rectify this, but in my experience all the really good classes such as Urban Street Dance and Combat Kick-Boxing will be full of young and fit 30-somethings. There will not be a saggy bottom in sight (except yours) and this will only serve to make you feel really crap.

Everything pointing southwards

I don't quite know what the science behind it is, but there's definitely something inexplicable going on when you make that transition from being a 30-something to a 40-something woman. One minute you're toned, pert and perky and the next you wake up and find that everything is pointing south. Why is that?

I do have a theory and that is that Mother Nature is again responsible for this. Not content with making us want babies, she then does all she can to ensure that we stick around and care for the babies she made us want to make. Her way of doing this is to wave her magic wand and make everything in our bodies droop southwards, so that there is no danger of us buggering off to the Bahamas in a thong bikini. I'm also sure that Bravissimo is in league with Mother Nature

about this, considering the amount of support bras
I have had to buy since I turned 40.

*Forty is the old age of youth;
fifty the youth of old age*

Victor Hugo

CHAPTER 6

THE ADVANTAGES OF BEING 40

You know you're 40 when...
you seem to have a lot more patience
now than before but the reality is you
just don't care.

Advantages? "Are there any?!" I hear you scream. Yes, of course there are, such as...well...um...oh yes, OK, what about the following:

Taking advantage of the young's stupidity

Do you remember when calculators made their mark on the world? As is the case with most new technological gadgets, people often found it easier and quicker to work out sums in their head than try to get said head around which button meant 'divide by'. Here is one advantage you have of being older than the average check-out girl at the supermarket and one that is great fun, particularly if you found a new grey hair that morning.

When the check-out girl tells you the amount for your groceries, for example seven pounds, forty eight pence, hand over a ten pound note and just after she's rung in ten pounds and has opened the till, smile and offer her the forty eight pence.

You can now sit back and watch, feeling very smug with yourself that she can't work out how much change she has to give you back and she can't ask the till to work it out for her either. Oh, the joys of having to learn maths without the aid of a calculator!

You will no longer get spots

Another advantage of getting older is that you will no longer have to go through the agony of acne ever again. With hot-flushes looming in the not too distant future, your skin will be glowing and blemish free for a good ten years ahead of you and you can laugh in the spotty face of the cashier who can't give out the right amount of change.

You have life experience

It's quite nice to watch people younger than you going through all the turmoil of growing up now that you've been there and done that. You no longer have to wait anxiously for the phone to ring or put up with a wonky fringe just because that's what all your friends' hair looks like. You don't have to pretend you're older than you really are in order to get into a pub and you no longer have that 'first date' panic, because you've already done that a hundred times over and are now qualified to give sage-like advice, such as, "There are plenty more fish in the sea," and "You are young, but you will learn."

Added to this, with 40 years' worth of life experience under your belt, you are now qualified to become a successful novelist, if you so choose. I mean, please. What publisher in their right mind is going to take on a 17-year-old whose only method of communication is, "WANNA MT UP L8R?"

You can say I told you so, a lot

And it's thanks to the 40 years' life experience that you can officially say, "I told you so" as many times as you wish and feel very self-righteous about it too because at your age you have most probably experienced, experimented and encountered every subject the young-uns have yet to go through. You know that if you drink alcohol on top of milk it does not actually prevent you from having a hangover the following morning; it actually makes you violently sick. You know that when he says, "I'll ring you" it really means that you won't see him for dust. And you know that a diet of pizza and coke will result in a painful gallstone that will have to be removed when you're 35.

You can officially rant and rave at people

Once you hit mid-life you are expected to turn into a wailing banshee, which is great because you can now shout and rant and rave to your heart's content and people won't bat an eyelid. You can officially insist on good customer service, demand as many free carrier bags as you like and tell the "Would you like to save money on your utility bills, madam?" salesman to naff off and get a proper job – all without being hauled off by security. Because this is what people expect us 40-somethings to behave like, so embrace it in all its banshee wailing glory!

Any idiot can face a crisis. It's the day to day living that wears you out

Anton Chekhov

CHAPTER 7

THE 40-YEAR-OLD AND KIDS

You know you're 40 when...

you finally get your head together,
but your body starts falling apart.

I thought it might be wise to dedicate this chapter to the life as a 40-something parent. It doesn't get much tougher than turning 40 and realizing that those adorable little pink humans, with the podgy arms and legs, have turned into ungrateful teenagers who habitually grunt in response to anything and everything and think that you're the oldest, uncoollest person on the planet who needs to stop nagging and get a life.

Yep, yet another thing we 40-somethings have to contend with... The angelic-looking child that you brought into the world and have selflessly dedicated the past 10-15 years of your life to is turning into someone who spends their time annoying you with daft questions or mumbling incoherently and sleeping a lot.

They will never be able to imagine that you, with your new-found grey hairs and wobbly bits, and unceasing tussle with gravity, were ever young. The fact that you can barely manage to turn on your mobile phone, let alone work out how to change it from predictive to normal text, only reinforces this belief. However, being that much older than your children entitles you to a few benefits...

As long as you live under my roof

Oh, finally to be able to say those words with authority! The fact of the matter is that because you pay for everything, including the central heating, the gas and electricity that they all take for granted, this fully entitles you to say the same things that your own mother said to you when you were younger. And you can always get what you want by threatening that if they don't like it, they can always move out. Unfortunately, they won't ever pack their bags due to the fact that they a) can't afford to because they are too damn lazy to get a proper job and b) they probably don't know how to pack for themselves yet. All in all it's a win-win situation for you – you get to tell them what to do and when to do it with the threat of eviction.

You are now also entitled to say things like "Would it kill you to walk three paces to the bin?" and "What time do you call this?" or "Do you really want to be working at McDonald's for the rest of your life?"

You can secretly become a techno-expert

Now, there's a method in this madness. In fact you don't even have to make it a secret because your kids won't be listening to a single word you say anyway. However, a few weeks at the I Can Do Technology Too class every Thursday night and you will have no trouble telling the difference between your RAM and your ROM. In fact, you will be so techno-savvy that it will be the kids who will be asking you how to multi-layer in Photoshop and, depending on your mood at the time, you can be the one to make dinosaur noises and say things like, "Durh, God, you're like soooo sad not knowing that!"

You can embarrass them in front of their friends

When it gets too much to handle, there's always the embarrass-and-humiliate option which always works a treat. There are many ways in which to embarrass your teenager; from dressing up in a mini-skirt and fishnet stockings for parents' evening and telling the Headmaster that you can't stay long as you have to get to work... to nicking their bike (or whatever rubbish method of transport they have because they are too young to drive – ha-ha) and whizzing up to them outside the youth club or wherever it is they hang out with their friends (because they're too young to go to the pub – ha-ha), blowing a whistle in their ear and telling them it's time to come in for their bath. It is your right as a parent to embarrass your children, so take full advantage of the fact that they hate you anyway, so what does it matter?

Age is a high price to pay for maturity

Tom Stoppard

CHAPTER 8

LIFE BEGINS AT 40!

You know you're 40 when...
you think coffee is one of the most
important things in life.

It may not feel like it now, but by taking a leaf out of the book of all those 40-something pioneering women, you can easily fool yourself into thinking that you can still do something meaningful with your life... All right, so it is not advisable to go crazy and attempt to climb Mount Everest, but life can begin at 40, or at least you can kid yourself it can.

So, here are some tips to support this theory...

Mirror, mirror on the wall

You may not look young and beautiful, but that doesn't mean you can't pretend you are. To help you feel like a million dollars, take down or cover up all the mirrors in your house so that you don't have to be reminded that you are older and greyer than usual. If, like me, you happen to live in a household with young and beautiful people that selfishly wish to admire how young and beautiful they are, simply stick a life-size photo of yourself from 20 years ago on to all the mirrors.

Positive thinking and all that

Lots of boffins in white coats with nothing better to do with their time have scientifically proven that positive thinking indeed helps us to achieve miracles. So whilst you're slapping on the Olay Definity and plucking the grey hairs that are standing to attention in line with your parting, you can sing positive affirmations, such as "I have no wrinkles and grey hairs!" and "Beneath this sagging body of mine, is a goddess bursting to get out!" I don't know whether this method works but, if nothing else, it will take your mind off your grey hairs.

Get yourself some older/uglier friends

In order to feel better about yourself it's advisable to drop any of your glamorous-looking 40-something friends like hot leg wax and sign up to become a member of the W.I, League of Friends or other such clubs that people with more grey hair than you frequent. This way you will look the best and youngest person in the joint, and you might just get to appear as Ms December on the Farmers' Wives nude calendar, even if you're neither married nor have ever been married (which is a bonus) to a farmer.

Cheaper holidays

Another advantage of being a 40-something is that you no longer have to tolerate those god-damn-awful Haven holiday camps with the little kids and can instead take yourself off to the Caribbean for a fortnight. After all, the teenage kids are always saying they want to be treated like grown-ups, so now's your chance to let them get on with it. Let's see if they can survive on a shopping budget of £60 a week, shall we?

Cheaper clothing expenses

And you thought it was all downhill from here on! Well, let me tell you, it just gets better and better. The older you get, the cheaper your wardrobe expenses will become because fashion has a habit of repeating itself every 25 years or so. So that monochrome, dogtooth jacket with the shoulder pads you bought back in the '80s will be back in fashion again, saving you a fortune in clothing expenses. Mind you, so will the luminous leg-warmers, the rah-rah skirt and the red fishnet tights, which looked ridiculous back then and will look ridiculous now. Please re-read chapter four.

It's sad to grow old, but nice to ripen

Brigitte Bardot

CHAPTER 9

THE SELF-HELP SYNDROME

You know you're 40 when...
you hope there's not too much
more to learn the hard way.

A common disorder of women who have just turned 40 is that we are constantly striving to find guidance and advice on how to look younger, feel younger, better ourselves and generally become more fulfilled with our lives.

There you are, one minute an invincible 30-something woman and the next day you find yourself getting out of breath just climbing the stairs. So, are self-help books all they're cracked up to be, or are we just deluding ourselves that we will be fitter, slimmer, less neurotic and happier in just seven days?

The self-help industry

The self-help section of the bookshop is where you will find other miserable 40-something women all in a desperate bid to find themselves, or at least someone a few years younger, fitter, slimmer and more confident than themselves.

Yes, look in any bookshop and there you will find, huddled in the corner of the self-help section, a 40-something woman on a mission to recapture her youth and freedom through a range of titles such as *You Can Do It If You Really Want*, which only reinforces our lack of self-esteem because it's like saying to someone, "Well, if you got off your 40-something lard arse the size of Wales, and actually put some effort in, you too could be as beautiful and fulfilled as me."

These self-help books and the *New Year, New You* articles that regularly make an appearance in the monthly glossy magazines are all designed to make us mere mortals feel like losers.

The self-improvement market is the U.S. is worth more than nine billion dollars and a quick search on Amazon reveals that there are over 20,000 titles available on self-help topics. A good 99% of these books are sold to the 40-something woman – the other 1% is probably purchased by the author's mum. Can you believe that over 40,000 people in the U.S. work as Life Coaches?

We're constantly being told to eat better but eat less, watch less TV but relax more, make more money but at the same time simplify our lives and stop being so materialistic, live prosperously but stop being so controlling but at the same time money doesn't bring us happiness and we should control our own destiny. It's no wonder we're all so messed up! A quick look at some of the recent self-improvement books available have titles along the lines of:

Change Your Life In A Matter of Days

Days? Is that all? It takes me longer to change my mind, let alone my life. How on Earth are you supposed to change your entire life in a month? Does this mean you just say bollocks to everything, chuck in your job, resign from your parental duties and stop taking responsibility for everyone else? Hm, could work.

I Did It, So Can You!

Well, good for you! The title alone just makes you feel like punching someone, doesn't it? Talk about kicking someone when they're down. Not only are we having to face the prospect of loosing our looks, our minds and having to rely on Tena Lady whenever we laugh, we're faced with some smug-arsed author who tells us how bloody brilliant they are and what a fantastic life they lead.

Face Your Fear And Just Do It!

Why on Earth would you wish to face your fears? Do you realize just how dangerous advice like this is? The feeling of fear is a natural inbuilt reaction to things that are dangerous to us. It's that old fight-or-flight thing we had when faced with the prospect of being eaten by a 50-foot Tyrannosaurus Rex – hm, face my fear and get my head bitten off, or outrun the bastard? We have fear for a reason – to keep us safe.

Self-improvement titles serve only two purposes: 1) to make you feel even more rubbish than you

already do and 2) to make the smug-arsed author
better off, happier, more materialistic and
contented about themselves.

With this in mind I have created my own top five
list of self-improvement titles for the 40-
something woman:

Number 1:

Release Your Inner Child And Give It A Good Slap!

For anyone who is convinced that releasing their
inner child is a good idea – it's not. Doing
cartwheels in the middle of the street is cute when
you're five years old. It's not when you're 40-
something. You will just end up looking like a
lunatic and, besides, being a child is rubbish. They're
not allowed to do anything and have to be in bed
by 7.30 p.m. *Release Your Inner Child And Give It A*

Good Slap! will be available at some point when I can be bothered to sit down and write it in between writing my funeral plans and heading off into town for the M&S sale.

Number 2:

So Michael Flatley Is Inside Your Head

This is the ideal gift for the 40-something woman who has discovered that the little Irish man tap-tapping in her head is actually her biological clock ticking. This easy-to-use guide will show you step-by-step how to recognize the signs and prevent a full ensemble of Irish dancers taking up valuable head space by finding a suitable man to have babies with.

Number 3:

Learn to Laugh At Yourself

And by this I don't mean that hysterical laugh that you develop every time you realize that it's all down hill from here on. If you can learn to laugh at yourself at least you will not feel so alone and depressed at the thought of being 40-something – although I do recommend that you do your laughing in the privacy of your own home. You might attract some unwanted attention if you point at your reflection and laugh every time you pass a shop window.

Number 4:

Do Nothing And Be Happy

It's very overrated all this trying new things, facing our fears, and spending hours trying to be the best at everything. *Do Nothing And Be Happy* does exactly what it says on the tin. Do nothing and you will never get disappointed again!

Number 5:

I Am Fabulous!

We all need to be told this on a regular basis and this is just what *I Am Fabulous!* does. Just to give you a boost every day, turn to any page in the book and it will tell you just how fabulous you are. What more do you need?

Regrets are the natural property
of grey hairs

Charles Dickens

CHAPTER 10

AT LEAST YOU'RE NOT 50

You know you're 40 when...

you would rather go to work than
throw a sickie.

See, there is light at the end of the tunnel. You may well have turned into someone who now has a passion for taupe-coloured M&S knickers and you may have started dressing like your mother, but at least you're not 50!

Not only does the 50-something woman have to contend with having more than a smattering of grey, more than an extra inch around her hips, and more than an emergency pack of Tena Lady, she has to put up with hot flushes and a weak bladder and just when she's finally managed to get rid of the kids, she feels too bloody exhausted to do anything remotely exciting or of interest.

You may well be feeling like poo at the thought of being a 40-something, but at least you don't feel like hot, runny poo and can still get on a bike without pulling every muscle in your body.

Unless you're Madonna of course, the poor 50-something woman is stuck in limbo – she can't retire because she's still too young, and yet she can't move forward in her job because she's considered too old to be retrained in anything. The minute she's managed to get rid of the kids is the minute they announce that they are pregnant and before she knows it she is up to her eyes in stinky nappies and regurgitated SMA again.

The 50-something woman is still too young to get all those freebies the 60-something woman is entitled to, such as great days out to Bournemouth for about £3.00 (meals included), and yet she's too old to hang out in a nightclub – unless of course she's Madonna or she wants to be known as that-crazy-old-woman-who-is-trying-to-recapture-her-youth.

You think you have it bad now. Think about the poor 50-something woman, resigned to watching repeats of *The Professionals* on UK Gold because she is stuck in that halfway house that is the world of the 50-something woman.

And if that didn't do it, think of games for the over fifties that you don't have to worry about for a while yet:

- *Sag, you're It*

- *Hide and go pee*

- *Twenty questions shouted into your good ear*

- *Musical recliners*

- *Simon says something incoherent*

Feel better now?

Fear not about avoiding temptation,
as you grow older, it starts avoiding you

Anon

CHAPTER 11

FORTY FACTS ABOUT ALL THINGS FORTYISH

You know you're 40 when...
You just can't remember who
shot J.R.

FACT 1:
40 is an octagonal number.

FACT 2:
The letters of the word forty are in alphabetical order.

FACT 3:
40 days and 40 nights was how long it rained for Noah.

FACT 4:
40 winks means a short sleep.

FACT 5:
40 years is the ruby wedding anniversary.

FACT 6:

Russian vodka is 40%.

FACT 7:

40 weeks is the usual number of weeks a woman is pregnant for.

FACT 8:

There are 40 hits in the UK charts.

FACT 9:

A rhinoceros' life span is 40 years.

FACT 10:

A hippo's is 41.

FACT 11:

Martin Luther King, James Dean and Marilyn Monroe all died before their 40th birthdays.

FACT 12:

It takes 43 muscles to frown, but only 17 to smile.

FACT 13:

The average length of a coat-hanger when stretched out is 44 inches.

FACT 14:
On average, 42,000 balls are used at the Wimbledon tennis tournament.

FACT 15:
The average cow produces 40 glasses of milk per day.

FACT 16:
There are approximately 45 billion fat cells in the average adult.

FACT 17:
40% of a human's weight is muscle.

FACT 18:

The Oscar statue design was changed in 1940.

FACT 19:

In 1940, actress Hattie McDaniel won an Oscar for her role as Mammy in *Gone With The Wind*.

FACT 20:

There are more than 40,000 characters in Chinese script.

FACT 21:

At -40°C a person will lose about 14 calories by just breathing.

FACT 22:
There are more than 40 different types of kangaroo.

FACT 23:
Mosquitoes have 47 teeth.

FACT 24:
40% of all McDonald's sales come from Happy Meals.

FACT 25:
Adults over the age of 45 eat the most ice-cream per person.

FACT 26:
In December 2008 the computer mouse celebrated its 40th birthday.

FACT 27:
John Lennon was born on October 9th, 1940.

FACT 28:
Sylvester Stallone's paintings sell for $40,000 each.

FACT 29:
40% of women in the U.S. were Girl Guides.

FACT 30:
You share your 40th birthday with nine million others.

FACT 31:
More than 40% of American households have guns.

FACT 32:
There are 42 dots on a pair of dice.

FACT 33:
There are 48 teaspoons in a cup.

FACT 34:
Sharks can travel up to 40 miles per hour.

FACT 35:
There are 40 different species of bats in the USA.

FACT 36:
In the Broadway version of *Beauty & The Beast*
more than 140 wigs are used.

FACT 37:
There are 40 different roles for male ballet dancers
in *The Nutcracker*.

FACT 38:

TV talk show host, Jay Leno, owns more than 40 motorcycles.

FACT 39:

Lawrence Olivier was knighted at the age of 40.

FACT 40:

The Hitchcock movie *Psycho* earnt more than $40 million dollars.

CHAPTER 12

KEEPING YOUR SENSE OF HUMOUR

The older I grow, the more I distrust the familiar doctrine that age brings wisdom

H.L. Mencken

A reporter was interviewing a 104-year-old woman.

"And what do you think is the best thing about being 104?" the reporter asked.

She simply replied, "No peer pressure."

Wisdom doesn't necessarily come with age.
Sometimes age just shows up all by itself

Tom Wilson

A woman walked up to a little old man rocking in a chair on his porch.

"I couldn't help noticing how happy you look," she said. "What's your secret for a long happy life?"

"I smoke three packs of cigarettes a day," he said. "I also drink a case of whisky a week, eat fatty foods, and never exercise."

"That's amazing," the woman said. "How old are you?'

"Twenty-six," he replied, grinning.

For the first half of your life people tell you what you should do. For the second half they tell you what you should have done

Richard Needham

Old academics never die...
they just lose their faculties

Old accountants never die...
they just lose their balance

Old archers never die...
they just bow and quiver

Old bankers never die...
they just lose interest

Old computer programmers never die...
They just byte the dust

*The really frightening thing about middle age
is the knowledge that you'll grow out of it*

Doris Day

THE SENILITY PRAYER

May I have the senility
to forget the people I never liked
the good fortune
to run into the ones I do
and the eyesight
to tell the difference

You know you're into middle age when you realize that caution is the only thing you care to exercise

Anon

A little old man shuffled slowly into an ice cream parlour and pulled himself slowly, painfully, up onto a stool. After catching his breath, he ordered a banana split.

The waitress asked kindly, "Crushed nuts?"

"No," he replied, "Arthritis."

If the young only knew...
If the old only could

French proverb

Herbert, an elderly gentleman, had experienced serious hearing problems for a number of years. He went to the doctor and the doctor was able to have him fitted for a set of hearing aids that allowed him to hear 100%.

Herbert went back to the doctor a month later for a check-up. The doctor said, "Your hearing is perfect. Your family must be really pleased that you can hear again."

Herbert replied, "Oh, I haven't told my family yet. I just sit around and listen to their conversations. I've changed my will three times!"

Two elderly couples were enjoying a friendly conversation when one of the men asked the other, "Fred, how was the memory clinic you went to last month?"

"Great!" Fred replied. "They taught us all the latest psychological techniques... it made a huge difference for me."

"Wonderful! What was the name of the clinic?"

Fred went blank. He thought and thought, but couldn't remember. Then a smile broke across his face and he asked, "What do you call that flower with the long stem and thorns?"

"You mean a rose?"

"Yes, that's it!" He turned to his wife...
"Rose, what was the name of that clinic?"

Inside every older person is a younger person...
wondering what the hell happened

Cora Harvey Armstrong

Geography of Women

Between 18 and 22, a woman is like Africa...
half discovered, half wild, naturally beautiful with fertile soil.

Between 23 and 30, a woman is like Europe...
well developed and open to trade, especially for someone with cash.

Between 31 and 35, a woman is like India...
very hot, relaxed and convinced of her own beauty.

Between 36 and 40, a woman is like France...
gently aging but still warm and a desirable place to visit.

Between 41 and 50, a woman is like Great Britain...
with a glorious and all conquering past.

Between 51 and 60, a woman is like the former
Yugoslavia...
having lost the war and haunted by past mistakes.

Between 61 and 70, a woman is like Russia...
very wide with borders now unpatrolled.

After 70, she becomes like Tibet...
*wildly beautiful, with a mysterious past and the
wisdom of the ages... only those with an
adventurous spirit and a thirst for spiritual
knowledge visit there.*

It's never to late to learn. But then if you've made it this far... why bother?

Anon

A recent survey showed that in their twenties 90% of men have sex four times a week and that by the time they reach 40 they are still capable of telling the same ridiculous lie.

We do not stop playing because we grow old.
We grow old because we stop playing!

Benjamin Franklin

If you enjoyed this book, please visit
www.crombiejardine.com
for others like it.

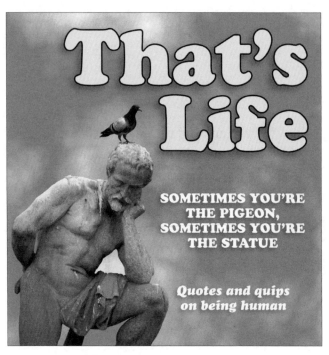

That's Life

SOMETIMES YOU'RE THE PIGEON, SOMETIMES YOU'RE THE STATUE

Quotes and quips on being human

ISBN: 978-1-906051-44-0, £7.99, HB

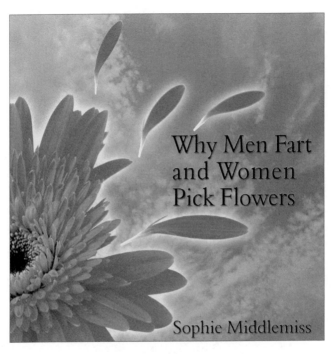

Why Men Fart
and Women
Pick Flowers

Sophie Middlemiss

ISBN: 978-1-906051-31-0, £7.99, HB

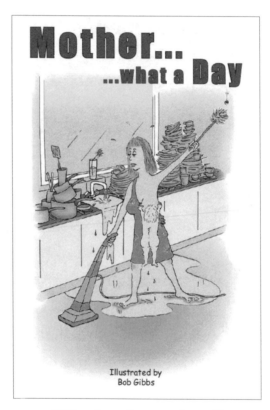

Illustrated by
Bob Gibbs

ISBN: 978-1-906051-01-3, £4.99, PB